The Matador's Wife

poetry + prose

by Andrés Colón

QUILLKEEPERS PRESS

Forward

The Matador's Wife represents many things to me. My relationship to domesticity, family, femininity; my navigation through Southern-Baptist sects, as well as my eventual escape from dogma. But *The Matador's Wife* isn't about me. *The Matador's Wife* is about crawling out of the rubble left behind from the self-destruction of someone you placed far too much faith in, someone (or something) that skewed your model of idealism. It is about the places we find ourselves when we remove the veils of our own innocence and allow for dull truths (the dull truth, for me at least, that I don't know many truths). I didn't want to write a story with heroes and villains, victims and perpetrators. Because more often than not, we behave much more reactionarily, adjacent to the "bigger picture" of things rather than at the forefront of them. This idea was much more intriguing to me. I wanted to write of the quiet violences. I wanted to write about things that end incomplete. Because it is always the silence that keeps me up at night.

"Many bulls surround me;
strong bulls of Bashan encircle me."
Psalm 22:12

His spite I keep in pickle jars
His love I keep in oil lights

Me and the dog, we lie,
stomachs up and just our fur
to hide us from the hypothermia.
And just our meat to keep us prized.
And just our bones,
just wrong enough to keep us in our places
in the basement of this hoarder's house.
Me and the dog, we lie like stillborns
below the anger of the Matador
on the first floor.
But when his anger drips from the first floor
we always know to catch it
before it hits the basement floor
to keep the wood from rotting.
The wood, already so wrong
with its latched fingers
and its nails at a point of breaking.
But this foundation is the only thing sacred.
And we are good girls
with old bones and new tricks,
so when we catch the anger that drips,
we pour it in pickle jars
to preserve his hissy fit
and keep it from spreading.
And we place the pickle jars with all the others
in the landfill of this hoarder's house.

I myself like to pretend that it's a pageantry—
which of the glasses can distort his spite
into something more lite?
A nice man, an ordinary man,
small towned and busy handed,
he's a misunderstanding that's great with questions.
But the glasses can only hold so little delicacy
and I, even less.
It's becoming cramped here in his clutch,
Matador, must you make matter of everything?

The Matador's Wife

Soot dusts my hands from tonight's kitchen fire
in preparation for the Matador's dinner.
My perfect, filthy mittens
for when desire brings callouses
and gets between the nailbeds.
Except, to be frank,
the soot that dusts my hands is more similar in shape
to the gloves of a chemist.
And to be frank,
I keep my hands dirty.
I keep the gloves on in case they cause me
to come upon something,
like a formula or a theorem
that explains the reasons you fuse,
why you scare the crops along with the crows, never to grow.
Or why you boil over the lip of the pot
and burn the very feet that carry you,
the very martyr that lays atop you to diffuse you.

I've shaved every place where you've been
so I can fit between the burweed
and not get caught.
I've begun wearing beige instead of red
to blend,
to bend with the tall grasses.
I've made myself small,
a little white rabbit.

You still dye me red;
and I wish you'd make me into a fur scarf
so that I can be the one to have your neck.
But I must shrink myself and all of my graces into oblivion,
into a horsefly of a wife,
if I'm not dead by next September.
I suck the water from my shirt
and prepare my prickly head for when you become the desert.
When is it that I became the Matador to the bull?
Must I make myself a wife?
If this is a wife, I shall never have a wife.

Cowboy in the New West Ghost-Town

The tornado sirens are tested every Wednesday of the month,
precisely at noon.
I forget this is routine on my route down main street
with my hand on my driver's wheel like a gun,
ready for a rodeo
or a shift in radio.
I thought the siren came from some road-rage
but I know I'm the last on earth
and I know I'm the only brave soul who would dare come
out the soil
while the hairs of these streets stay tucked away in their follicles
and its inhabitants go ingrown in their homes.
There are packing peanuts instead of petals
and a plastic bag like a tumbleweed.
There are fires that fall red yellow and green
instead of the leaves.
Sporadic is the new normal, it seems
in this spore-less spring.

I'm reminded of when
the pores of the street were clogged to the seams
like my car's compartments
where I keep my drumsticks and CDs.
They tremble along to these apocalyptic obsessions
as I reach lightspeed.
I suppose this is spring.

The park swings move capriciously

yet they are empty and without any child to rock them.

I wonder how this can be.

Then I remember it must be the breeze

for

the tornado sirens are tested every Wednesday of the month,

precisely at noon.

Words I keep in my left boot
(on longs walks)
#1

There's a house in my neighborhood where a boy was
shot. His parents decorate their lawn with a new
ornamental in his honor every year. I've never seen the
grass below the memorial, I'll never know if it's still
green. Their grief overgrows the ivy, and their plants
are all rotten, but I know that this pile of porcelain and
glass and picture frames and brass is their garden.

All You Touch in Falling

I meet him at his lips.
And he tastes like metal
like there's something corrosive in his core.
He brushes against me
like he's trying to strike a match.
He pretends he's understanding
when I make him show me the fire escape,
just in case.
His touch doesn't feel so self-righteous anymore.
My ears pop like a gunshot
to this derby race.
His passion erects into aggression
and I become so heavy
I fall straight through me.
I try to tether myself
because I know a kite without strings
is just skin with a stubborn backbone.
I wish that I was seventeen
when I thought I'd make it out of anything.
But this isn't coming out the sheets
for the life of it.
I don't think I've ever felt so empty
while entirely full of somebody.
I think of another the whole time.

I think of how my mother hates her body
and how when she was pregnant with me
I probably made her look unflattering.
I think of this man before me in his innocence,
before he became a stereotype.
Before, when he swore he'd never stare at me
like this.
I think this as he wraps me up inside of him,
like a babe.
If you could call it that, and not just consumption.
There is no nurturing here—
he uses spit instead of baby oil
or vaseline at least,
and he keeps his cleaning supplies
on the bottom shelf, within my reach.
These are not signs of someone
who will ever be a father
and it's days like this I wish I'd stayed
inside of my mother.

Words I keep in my left boot
(on longs walks)
#2

Every evening I used to balance on curbs
to make myself linear
and walk between yellow lines
to feel confinement.

Moon's Craters

I only knew there to be three things: the Sun, the Moon (me), and unfinished business (this thing between us called Space, like a place under the bed where we were dropped). I only knew there to be three things until a fourth thing appeared behind me—a tick on my back named Apollo. How disappointed I was to hear he wasn't the driver of the Sun. Because I wanted a collision that day. And that's to say I wanted company. I wanted some of the Sun's imagery to refract. But someone's son stood on my back. Apollo said he was Apollo Eleven and I said, "is Eleven the thing that stands in line behind Four? And how can One of you be Two? Is there no space between Eleven and you?" And to that he said, "Actually, there is space. There is a single space, a single place to house a single Breath." I apologized because Breath is homeless here. "It's quite alright" he said, "I've got my own orbits" as he pointed to his Helmet, which orbited Breath, which orbited Head. And he placed a foot in me, but I was used to craters. Then he placed a flag pole in me. As if I was someone to be discovered. A flag with his primary colors—red white blue. And he called himself the Man on the Moon. As if I were a groom with a surname worth excavating. But I was used to craters.

Man's Craters

I only knew there to be two things: to omit or to amend. So, if a question is a crater and if there is no answer to fill it, then like any good globe maker, I must hollow a hole out of it to put a pole through it, like any good jouster. So, I ask hollowly: What erosion bruised the Moon? And what asteroid ran from home? And what split up its pack like wheat from the shaft? The wheat from the shaft that collides with an eye during seasons dry. An eye with a crater where light refracts imagery, like the Moon. Imagery of colors primary—red yellow blue. How scary it seems to be granted to see. The eye, yet another planet the Sun rubs. The Sun, a lecherous one. But let selfishness not become me, for I need remember that it is generous of the Sun to let us see him; as they say "the Sun is up therefore I am up". But I know he only does this out of loneliness, in the way divinity is often full of it. And as the ego of dawn overcomes the Sun, it dawns on me: company is a collision with years between connections. And years, to say, light-years. Take that as you will. But why size time to a meterstick? That's another crater to fill. We've got other time to kill.

Cartography

There is a man you know the way a cartographer knows
new soil. You keep your mappings quiet, not to be selfish
but to be sufficient. This could be a sanctuary if done
correctly. And no one else could notice and name every
organism and change in his landscape like you. Like the
way his linen shirt lifts when he stretches next to you,
revealing another layer of earth. Of your earth, this one
bristled in hairs and other blade-of-grass-like things. No
one could be an Adam to creation like you. So, five days
a week you'll place down your footprints till you find the
lowlands where the down-trip makes your ankles weak.
That is when you'll know you've struck groundwater.
And from there you'll dig not like a cartographer or an
excavator, but like a painter. To preserve. To capture. But
not like a zookeeper, like a painter, remember, to get the
full picture; for he, he is omnipresent. You'll dig to the
point of no return. And here you'll plant yourself,
because what else? And here your roots will spread and
you'll become the land and you'll become the man,
because how else? Oh, you'll spread alright. But not the
way you're used to spreading. Not like the tide of desire.
Not like the hubris of an empire. And not like the
distribution of limbs across skin either, nor the heat that
lies beneath. This will be a different heat. This will be the
kind of damnation that's branded. Because you'll dig this

dirt into a grave. You'll dig this dirt till what's left of it between your nails is incriminating, spreading, like every stain on his linen. And you'll wonder if you're not so different from him. And you'll never feel so small. So small you could camp out in his ear canal for just a sip of his subconscious. You never wanted to know a man this closely, you'll promise.

But once, "*it was very good.*"
Genesis 1:31

Johnny Appleweed vs. the Dumb Gum Tree

They knew me as Johnny Appleweed with evil stuck
between my teeth
and my teeth were seeds with roots like weeds that grew
into a dumb gum tree
and from the dumb gum tree hung a swing
and on the swing swung lil' ol' me
and from lil' ol' me came a push for speed
—so high I knocked my knobby knees on the high high
branch of the dumb gum tree
and so the tree put a splinter in me
and right out of me came a wee ol' scream
—it wasn't the "wee!" I expected there to be
when it came to swings
and so off my swing I walked it off, you see, I let the splinter be
and from letting it be it grew into a stake, like the back of a bee
and so like a bee I used it to sting, the evil in me became
the evil out me
and I planted the seeds of the evil of me all across Ohio wheat
and the wheat was chewed between my teeth till it got stuck
like the splinter in me
and they knew me as Johnny Appleweed with evil stuck
between my teeth.

Evil is the song of The Rattlin' Bog.
I swear to no longer sing along
or carve my revenge in fallen logs
for a wounded dog gets mean.

Arsonist

Follow the trail
across the cobbles,
down the coils
of my body's hair.
I grow it long
like one of your women.
I grow it long like ivy
and I let it cover me.
It draws out a cadence in your exhale
like a humble gale
against my windowsill.
So follow the trail
from the gutter to the dail.
Uproot the doornails
that lie beneath the ivy.
Use the beds of your nails.
See what entails
in my house made of shale.
I don't care what it costs me.

I showed you my body like a hoarder's basement;
like a hedge maze with a minotaur with no way out his cell
so he burns it all down
by rubbing together the sticks that he's found.

Dearest, you're an arsonist
but I'm an accomplice
and I'll never tell.
Oh, I'll never tell.
I'll be a time capsule,
tending to your warmth,
and I'll never tell.

Vegetable

I've never broken a bone
but I trust that you know
you can't see earth's curve
as you fall from the top of the tire swing.
So I suppose this flat world has its ends
because you said.
But was the skepticism
worth aging me in worry?
I hand over the bandage
and I'm looking for Jesus
in the palms of your hands,
picking the mulch
from where they'd nailed him.
I can't help but wonder,
would you have died for me
like I'm your biggest conspiracy?
I'd make you mud pies
if you could try them,
if I didn't have to pull all your teeth
with your brother's pliers.
You tell me I'm too sweet.
I push you again and you scream
higher higher higher.
We hide behind
the chatter of the washer and the dryer.

When I'm this close I can see
that there sprouts a hair from your chin
and it hits me,
you're to be a man of God,
so you love me frugally.
Sneaking me
through the window
like I'm your biggest conspiracy.
I called you out on that,
you let me hit you as payback.
God, I hate this sin but I love this sinner.
Then we're playing cops and robbers,
you'd learned it from your father.
Don't you know you aren't invincible?
I can't watch you become a vegetable.

When I went to your baptism
I thought that you were drowning.
I didn't know what the pastor meant
when he said it was by grace
that you would never be
the person you were before the cleansing.
But that's when I knew this flat world
had its endings
as you'd said to me,

because I would have forsaken
all of God's creation
if it meant I'd get your former self;
your wretched, your evil,
your rotten, bastard self.

He Says to Me

with a flashlight shined beneath the sheets:

"If you believe in a God, you've probably been asked about their maker, their matriarch—the umbilical cord that bridges a blood cell to an edema swell.

The lower-case g upheld its umbilical cord above its head, born out of its tangle and claustrophobia, and became the uppercase G—god became God.

and 'God' added on 'od', because how odd! But actually, 'od' is defined as:
'a hypothetical power once thought to pervade nature and account for various phenomena, such as magnetism.' Now that's odd.

And it is here I find myself cradled in hypotheses. Great power I have. Pain and power, a common magnetism. Like the primordial birth of a God. The force of it. Like harvesting a stone. The pain and power of a childbirth. It's 'labor' for a reason. We do not live in non-fiction. Conscience is a sci-fi.

And so if you believe in a God, you ask about the womb they came from. But what if it were the opposite? What if God did not stumble out of a cavern but into one? Like a fissure awaiting a river, a rock split without erosion. Not everything is made sewn together. Is a daughter cell not whole once it divorces its telophase?

Actually, let me not use the word 'divorce'. Not everything is a tragedy. Or carnal. Not everything is born in blood. Or born at all. Silence has no prelude. So why should I assume a God has a mother to miss? That the world began with a split? Who is who to assumes that there is always a 'who'? We are not planets. We have no orbits. Except, maybe we do…
But regardless;

What if God fell into?

Not 'in two'.

Into.

What if a God fell into the fissure of Nothing (if Beginning was Nothing) like a river,
and God was not the sailor but the water.

If you believe in a God, you're asked what cloud they came from, as if something came. As if there is always conception.

I don't blame the conspirators. I would be a hypocrite if I did. For there is no concept to this without a question…

So, if you believe in a God, what if they were a question? What if there was no answer…"

~~What if God Was a Silence? Everything That Isn't? Just~~
~~Negative?~~
~~A Title? No Body? Spineless?~~
~~What if I Stayed Silent?~~ ————————————— ~~I Think it'd~~
~~Look Something Like This.~~

And once, "*it was very good.*"
Genesis 1:31

A Furnace

I was never as honest
as your Jesus thought I could be.
I could never be a martyr.
I can't bring myself to believe in anything.
But there's something in my hair
and it's turning it to strings.
There's something, pulling, always something.
I want to believe that you see something in this fire that's burning
beyond my worries
because anything could be the end.
It could cut my flesh
with the same warmthness of your breath
and I'd draw my last.
I hope you see a furnace and not scorched forests.
I hope you see a wreath above it
and books beside it
with a security in their spines to brazen the blaze
and know that they are safe.
I hope you see a purity
that I have yet to know.
I want to know my barren feet on barren plains
without knowing the names that bear its graves.
I want to know your weight around me
without knowing it could drown me.
I want to believe in many things,
I want to believe that you believe in me.

Hermit Crab Dichotomies

I'm hanging on that wedding day.
I come across the vase from our sand pouring ceremony.
I think that it's the first desert we built for the two of us.
And slowly I go through it.
My sorting is studious;
…jagged…tusk mold…
…striped…an orifice…
…honeycomb gold…
…glass nucleus…
…this one's old…
…stone so rubious…
Have you ever seen sand up close?
It looks much like this,
like a village of rocks and shells shelved door to door.
I wish I could become a resident—a hermit in the shell bits—
to all my precious things,
my porous little things.
So I make my sorting studious, shifting the grains of sand
from hand to hand
like dice with a chance
as if it will land me a better land.
Cause I'm still hanging on that wedding day:
someone's baby was waiting for the band to stop their play.
Tell me, what were her first words, buried behind the bass?
And which will be my last?

I've been in this sand
for 40 days & 40 nights,
deserted in dichotomies,
sorting grands of the same sand
from our sand pouring ceremony
with my shovel hands,
searching for the grander scheme of these things.
And it's with these 2 hands I grasp that
when you have a left arm and a right arm
with no collar to bridge them,
when you have an embrace with no friction for his warmth,
when you curtain the sun with no dusk or dawn…
When you separate the land,
you have nowhere to stand.
You have nowhere to stand
except for your own sentiments
and you fall through the hole between the sediments.
And you make yourself a home in which your crabbiness
hermits.
And you must escape
because in the grand scheme of things
the tide will flood the sand village by the next minute.

Piñata

Woke from a dream in which you'd left me
suspended in strings
on the yard of your birthday.
And I'm cradling my sweetness within me
the way a kid tends to his balloon.
Will I deflate or slip into / in two?
Or will I just burst
at the sight of you?
My touch is so embarrassing / yours is so annihilating.
And I cannot brittle myself.
So I wait one more year
for my boy to come on his birthday,
batted and bruised,
and show me my goods.
Show me I'm good.
So I wait
for you to bring your weight
and for the gate
to no longer separate the caged from the free,
the jam from the jar,
the hand and the scar.
Don't make me beg for you
just because you know how to,
battled and bruised.
But with one more year,

you clutch the bat not like a boy
but like a man,
like a roof holds its weathervane
as if the wind is out to get him.
As if I held what was left of his adolescence inside of me,
in the sense that what's left of the sandbox
gets put in the hour glass.

Woke from a dream in which
you swung at the tree instead of at me,
and down came me along with your tire swing.
In place was a spout that sprouted the sap
of the tree. She's much sweeter than I'll ever be. And me,
with my goods gone stale.
But who cares about a fire when the house is vacant?

Words I keep in my left boot (on longs walks) #3

Picture me.
Shoot me
in photography.
Let me be
the dear in your headlights
this once.

Snaps

I want to believe your horses
when they whisper to me
of the places you've been,
like the crazed girls in paperbacks.
But I would never hear the end of it.
I could never fit your litanies on
my paper-thin back.
Tell me, is that why you stretch the skins
of girls between the maple trees
like hammocks to lie in?
Girls, sturdier than I.
I, who slants with the snap peas
and submits to the wind
and hears horses,
tell me.

**Words I keep in my left boot
(on longs walks)
#4**

This house is a place where my best friend cannot visit me,
she cannot see me with a man so much like her father.
And for that I am sorry.

little spoon

I sit within a dusted frame as a little souvenir spoon on a wall
of all the places that you've been.
And when the little spoon next door comes over and you fork her,
I'll let my sterling silver be the glimmer where she can rest her
rolling eyes
before she meets her demise
and becomes the prize that hangs beside me,
because I'm a good neighbor.
And I'll welcome her as a part of the map
on the wall of all the places that you've been.
And me and her will welcome the next girl after you map her back,
and the three of us will root for the girl after that
as you unsheathe your silver tongue, all sharp like a knife, and
show it to her,
because three's a crowd
and we are good neighbors.
And four spoons could make a feast
of boiling soup
that could finally fill you
and burn you too.
So that's what we'll do the next time you hold your little spoons
and little spoons hold boiling soup
and burn you too.
It's the least we can do as the littlest of spoons.

Taxider me

12:53

You lie next to me like it's an apology
and I've been having
a staring contest with your outlet
waiting for it to swallow me.
This room is never bare
with all the wallcoverings
and the cracks beneath.
I could never be permanent here.
No matter how much I stain,
there's always a springtime
to freshen up the paint.

1:05

I bring my eyes to your back,
and try to remember the first time I died.
It'd be romantic to lie
and imagine it felt a little bit like this.
Because soon you'll roll over me
and pat me down,
looking for parts of me that do not exist.
But your weight has yet to fully crush
and you would never commit so much
nor would you have me in my flesh
unless caught dead.
It'd be the first time you die.

1:23

Am I pulse?
Am I meat?
Am I plush?
Tell me what I mean.

1:26

You have your lips below my chin
and I wait for you to build the bridge.

3:16

You masturbate in your sleep,
exhaling a name I do not know.
There's a hesitation in your breath
as if you're contemplating how much oxygen this room has
left for the two of us.

3:17

This blanket covers me
and I crack beneath.

4:17

I hope I'm who you want me to be
in your dream
in your dream.

4:36

I hope your parents come home
so I can have a witness
to the crimes you might commit.

5:04

There's a pale blue light
outside of your window.
I pray it comes with sirens
to break my silence.
But it's only the swift-hand ferryman and
he's got a bone to pick with me;
I haven't been picking up the phone lately.
Although, the dog's been dying downstairs,
maybe he'll come for her instead.

Now I lay me down to sleep

I don't have to like the things you say at times.
I don't like the things I say.
What I keep from you is my weaponry,
nothing cuts like what you
don't know about me.
I've never felt more lonely than when you hold me
like a stray with a leg that limps,
there is no warmthness to your sympathy.
You're not with me when you're next to me,
but I let you sleep so I can scream.
I think you find me disgusting
but I know I bring the heat.
And I want to see your house aflame
but it's soundproof walls have kept you tame
and everything I ever did
was just another way to put your surname
to all my keepsakes.
I'm never cooking up what you crave.
But you're not mine to rectify
you're not mine to lose.
So I forget my name and lose my faith
to a dead-man's eyes and his swollen lips.
I almost drowned with the lakeside ships.
Don't you know
you could crush me in your fingertips,
right where the whole world sits.

It's hard to hide
the girl behind your hair.
And I'll never be there
I'll never be.
Girls aren't so hairy,
or so you say to me.
One day you'll kill me.
One day you'll keep me.

But I don't have to worry

because the next day I get word that the bull has won
and my Matador has went missing on the job,
supposedly.
I can't believe a thing
he does and doesn't say to me.

Double Dog Dare [empty chair]

Rat
Rattle Rat,
I scurry to set the table
as my knuckles
tap the armrest of my dining chair
like a gong, initiating a challenger's song.
I double dog dare you
to take me on
and all that I've become:
Godless, desperate, a jowl full of spit.
And there, across you sit:
an empty chair, peach, a pit,
you've outgrown your silence.
I'll pull the velvet tablecloth
and make this chair a chariot.
This womb will be my armor,
your daughter is a fighter,
her daddy is a goner.
Just ask the cops.
Or take none of this
and leave me to the epilogue,
but you're nobody's Goliath.
I double dog dare you
to take me on.
Can't you see this house is gorgeous

despite its bad back
and jutting hip
and silence?
I take a sip...
I'll pry that throat like loosening a cave and mine
those truths I'll pay no mind
to a broken tooth
I'll I'll
I'll.
I will till I'm ill.

I'm No Moses

Father who art in heaven,
hollowed is thy name.
I'm mounting this mountain,
and my finger is a rod, a battering ram to a gate.
I've become my own expulsion, I've bottled all the rain.
I've slit my hem I've made myself a blind
I've walked the coals I've burnt the bread
and stomached it too.
I have my heathens.
What more can I lose?
And what more could you?
Let me be the one that they believe in
who fills every refrain
and has heathens.
Get off the reigns.
Be off with your head.
Let me watch from overhead.

But I'm only debating an overhead light,
and this mountain is only a shag staircase.
I supposes
I'm no Moses.

I Break Plates (Eve)

I've felt God once.
I'd gotten too close to him with my questions;
so much so I'd broken my nose.
It was a winter,
and the wind turned its back to the window
as if to take no part in my defiance.
But that once, my questions were the closest I got
to some apostasy,
and apostasy is the most honest divinity
for a daughter.
I break plates to see if father notices that there's a chair at
the table missing.
That winter, the Christ considered me like a wolf considers
a hound.
And the hour was industrial and sexless,
with my knees scraping against
the sharpest of bedsheets
to hold what would ever be
the holiest of ghostings.
God was a parody if not a paradise,
and if there's a next time,
I'll be paying in dimes.
What if God Was a Silence?

Words I keep in my left boot
(on longs walks)
#5

I know that I write like I'm trying to prove my innocence
for crimes that I know that I've committed, I know.

Day-Lit Indolent

I wear the same thing as yesterday
and wring it out for any leftover thrills—
a laugh
a hiccup
or pollen
to wring a sneeze out of me
or something.
And soon it'll join the others,
all the clothes collecting on my floor.
This has become a habit at its core.
A habitat, really,
with subtle growth
and rained on often.
And it'll go on until my clothes overgrow the window
with the view of my childhood swing-set.
Because I believe life begins and ends with me
and I could never keep a houseplant alive,
though I swore I could hold up the sky.
There must be a woman in me somewhere.

I wear the same bed as yesterday,
I swaddle myself to become something else—
innocent, unborn,
an oyster.
It's become receding, wrinkled.
I'll cover it with the top sheet, say it's made.
I don't fit in my palms anymore.

I suppose I'm selfish for wanting something of my own.
I'm just a child wanting a child to mold—
something stationary and arbitrary,
something that can't stand on its own
or strengthen its legs
or denounce my name.
I should never be a mother,
I think I'd become my mother.

I wear the same room as yesterday.
Nobody has lived here before me
and I think I'm becoming its ghost stories.
I should never be a history.
I'm embarrassed of how they'll remember me
so I don't know why I keep screaming
but at least I'm in control of what it is
that will make them want to forget me.
I hope my dog forgives me
for letting her see
the rust consume the swing.

Night-Trip Nitwit

I go out with a bang
that's been bleached to an ivory
to dull down the stains
and my notoriety.

and I book an inn just to stay inside.
The hinge creaks but it refuses to close
though I'm not so alone when my
clock becomes my metronome.

And I don't have to worry if I'm aging or just disengaging,
because I can make up my own holidays
to plan my getaway to places like these
where I'm always greeted with bouquets and
everything is clean and even if I become the mess to clean,
the towels are free.
Places like these where I can hide from birds of prey,
still desperate for my decay.

Words I keep in my left boot
(on longs walks)
#6

I'm only important when I am not,
I'm only a parable when I extort my past.
I would recycle myself a hundred times over
if it gave them the correct correlations
and the best of my graces.
They'll get this wrong too.

I dream of silkworms, I dream of poisonous things

You invade my sleep
like how you invade temples in my dreams
full of smoke and covenants.
And in those dreams, you're a big god
and my body is a temple.
And every single night is another of your crimes
that I can't beat
cause in my sleep, history rhymes
but doesn't repeat.
Sometimes I dream of silkworms sewing limbs,
repairing where you've been
and absolving phantom pain.
Sometimes I dream of Datura's flowering
with all the other vespertine.
And I think it means
prosperity
and reclaiming my poisoning.
But I also dream
that your mouth is filled with foam
and you turn to salt between my teeth
and I cast you out into the sea.
I dream of church services and man-made havens
and then someone breaks in
and puts bullets through the bulletins.
I dream that I drag you from a burning building
but you feel like my foot when it falls asleep,
all heavy, as if you're stuck to something.

Stuck to other kisses, other couches
like a penny; treasure hunting in the cushions for conquests
more exhilarating,
more annihilating.
And I think you'd rather burn than be held by me.

I move to the couch to sleep
and press into the cow-brown leather in my living room.
There is nothing living here
with this much carnage,
cow skin and girl skin, we're pressed cheek to cheek.
My dog licks the armchair like the leather's still alive and
full of meat
till she falls asleep.

i

It's within a fogged-up mirror that I begin to feel myself
in minimalism:
my jaw and its twitch, just within a 4/4 timescale;
the crest of my head, crowned brown;
the scar below my brow, it's fading
like my outline's edges, all alien,
landing in the crop circles, my sacred plain.
I trace me with my fingers, scarred and lemon-peppered;
kneading my needs,
I customize me,
I compromise me.
Elasticity, ecstasy;
I'm so stretchy
I could freefall.

It's within a fogged-up mirror,
and I guess I've always expected peace to come to me
on the verge of something,
like a canyon or a concept or the wind before a storm forms…
but the closest edges here are these bathroom tiles
and their grout
and their history with my blackouts.
The memories make my stomach tight.

So, I knock on my navel with the courage of a drunk
to confront me at my core,

my belly button peephole,
like Alice through a keyhole
¡like an upside-down exclamation!
I used to be fed through here.
Now I'm led here
through its hallway.
My stomach caves,
my intestine snakes.
And it tells me, Eve, to be angry every eve
in order to scare the night-time creeps
so I can sleep in peace.
How tempting.

I think about going to bed earlier. My pride from having the
thought keeps me up later.

Goatskin

Your boots still sit in my backseat and when I come to
stops, they kick against me.
Horse-drawn, I proceed.
I'm more restless and threadbare than they will ever be.
The boots, they're your father's, they're your favorite,
they're my least.
They're the only things my moths can't eat.
But I won't, I won't get rid of them,
I couldn't afford the poster ink.
But that isn't the only thing.
For one, I know better than to pass on a cursed thing.
For two, a deed won't convince me I'm forgiving
or good in the least.
For three, the things I have loved I believe I can keep.
And I remember you, as put together as a fisher,
with the boots too big,
you stood firmly in your goatskin.
I knew nothing of insurance but I knew how to work a splint,
ready for when you'd break yourself in.
From the look of it,
you could've been your father, you could've been Huck Finn.
Boyish, your ambition couldn't catch a thing
except the attention of everyone
in sight of your shortcomings.
My mother has never liked you but forgive her,
I'm not so sure she's ever liked me.

And you're not really as radical as you think
but Maverick, if you're a coward then that makes two of us
who refuse to let the lake moss touch the bottoms of our feet,
floundering at the softer things.
Besides, I think I quite liked the mysteries of the deep, even
if it left me floating
cicada-like:
with a sight I'd never seen below
and with you right next to me.
And my head, somewhere.

Your boots still sit in my backseat and somewhere,
when your soles, your grievances,
when they've both worn to the bone,
know your boots will stand
if I can't, if I won't

Juggernaut

I drive this egg-white juggernaut
with my itty muscles taut
and the passenger's seat with sweets and beets
and all my other groceries bought.
From the back booster-seat kicks and screams
the bratty needs of an intrusive thought:

> *"Boy, these roads are quite the taboo for the mother of you*
> *cause she's got the clue that you'll do a corkscrew*
> *and end up crashed and askew like gran and gramps and*
> *Diana too…"*

I just keep jugging along in my egg-white juggernaut
so the jugs of white eggnog don't go all rot
like this same old rhyme that I've dragged on a lot;
a sign—not white—says that I must stop.

On the count of three and an adjusted seat I continue
onto helix roads that twist like DNA.
My family DNA calls my name like there ain't
plenty of dames to talk to in heaven's paradise.
This parasite still keeps its eyes on the hereditary way all
my family dies.
But these days DNA stands for Do Not Answer.

So, I DNA my DNA
as I approach a dead end.
This curse of my dead ones ends
with me and my curled dead ends.

Our ends are prewritten;
our obituaries sit in with the wills within
the family safe. But I've just got back my will
to keep myself safe, like I've finally found life's thrill…
well, this is quite the thrill.

Within this egg-like juggernaut my fiber
seatbelt gets tighter, like the umbilical cord
that killed baby Piper.
I bet my grasp is even tighter around the wheel of the driver
as my tires wheel around a turn much tighter.

I'm not that much of a daredevil cause I'm much too scared
of hell and its devil and
I can't take any more rants from my dead aunts
so I move my hand to turn up the dashboard's amp

and then dashes forth a man.

I shoulda got mom's clue cause I do a corkscrew
with the white lines in view

through the window that I jam through, with my cherry jam too.
I hatch from my egg-like juggernaut
and I'm newly yolked on the newly paved road
like a skillet…
well, I guess I'm well-done
with my grocery bags undone
and all over me, I'm a sandwich for one.
A sandwich for the shame of the j-walker to dine on.

At least, this is what the intrusive thought foretells to me
from the back booster-seat
on my drive home from the grocery.

Words I keep in my left boot
(on longs walks)
#7

In the winter, I'm shirtless,
in the summer, I'm skinless.
Shedding my layers to feel the extremes
to their every degree
so they can hit me beneath my necessities.
The bears in hibernation aren't here to question me
or think strangely of me, anyway.

Over the Counter

The touch screen blinks
as I channel surf for empathy.
I replay the MP3s I used to have him
send to me
to prove that he was real.
Because faith requires no sight but all sound.
And though my boy is not the voice in these sextapes,
if I turn them up they might intimidate
or take up some space
next to all this nothing
and touch me through the touch screen
like I'm 3D,
erected, stepped in, seen.
I'm drilled deep like a medicine cap;
desire is the hand I twist with
or just rattle the pills with.
These timestamps and their stimulation,
I must archive this.
I've learned the art of pressure and sinking,
of conforming to the static
and the weight of a room
where I can let my hair down
and let my lips salt.
These films don't watch back in the dark.
In dark, on screen, she's over the counter,
with a knack for improv only I could recognize.
I bet she thinks she's like the breadcrumbs

and he'll wipe her off his chin with his handkerchief.
And after, I know she'll
lather the beestings in aloe
and put herself up to dry.
I know, I know.
It's like watching chickens fight
yet I can't look away because I think I might find
some evidence
for a case of my own.
She knows, she knows.

Aviation

My boy was my Bermuda.
I remember once,
his momma told me I shouldn't have flown so close to her son,
and honestly, I can't quite recall all it is he did to me.
But in my aviation and my full-fueled zealot ways,
I see it quite plain,
barren, bloody plain.
If you teach your boys to start their gardens with plows,
if you train your boys to kiss with teeth,
as if fetching for a bone beneath tender meat,
he'll never know a wife like she knows herself.
And he'll never know the company she keeps
in her cupboards, full with the most domestic dust-bunnies.
He'll never know a mother like she knows herself,
or the paths she makes soft to keep her daughter's knees
from knocking;
the paths she makes soft for her man's safest landing.
So come home knocking.
Come home knowing it's a home and not just
a barren, bloody plain.
Not just the hospital bed where your daughter never formed.

I see it quite plain,
barren, bloody, plain.
But I'm not the Red Baron,
though I've struck some armies down.

And I'm not much like Amelia,
I've not yet made it out the West;
but I'm still thrashing to the ground,
lost in transmission.
My obsessive retrospection
is like kerosene that fogs the screen,
blurring my translations.
And I'm never to be found.
Just another pilot down.
But still I thrash
and bright I burn.

How to Dispose of a Dead Bird
(before the flames get in)

The rug you rip from under me fits nice and snuggly
over my dead head like a sack;
not like a kidnapping, but like plastic wrapping, all preserving.
Like the way a stepped-on bird gets put in its own plastic bag
like a little display case
so all can see when it joins the junkyard scene.
Like how the embryo of a bird's egg is also see-through,
and the bird in the plastic bag gets a final bit of babyhood
before the waste facility flames eat it through.

This body bag feels like babyhood,
but before I'm born again and the flames get in,
won't you hold my neck like I'm a bird again?
Won't you be my accident?
I'd look good on your walls
all soft
under fluorescents
all soft.
Poacher, who is there without the spotlight?
Without your red-dot sight and your immovable pride?
Poacher, won't you handle me at least?
Make me into something?
All crumbled between a plastic bag display case
and your killer face.

Give me a little lively thing.
Give me an embryo, remember me.
Show me everything that I can be
before the flames get in.

Double Dog Dare [empty chair] (Reprise)

Rat
Rattle Rat,
I scurry to set the table
as my knuckles
tap the armrest of my dining chair
like a gong, initiating a challenger's song.
Tonight it's me and me
and I know that she
is always down to take me on
and all that I've become:
a two headed viper with a hunger
for the soft ripe skull of the other.
I spit and I spit
and spit and then spit.
Tomorrow is the same
and so is the next day.
It is then that I sit,
I've outgrown this silence.
And my words only stick to the empty seat across from me
like a tongue to chilled metal.
It appears that the empty chair chose truth over dare.
And the truth of it all is that I mustn't see the drought
between the two halves of me
as a desert arena
like Jacob would
to rematch Yahweh.

And I mustn't see my flooding within
as another fish-filled sea
like Jonah would
to hide in.
And when I say that I'm the only one who can take me on,
I mustn't mean with a clenched fist
but with an open palm
because I cannot punch a boulder up a hill.
Simply, I sit and think
I am not my greatest enemy.
I would know that if I had listened to me,
for one half of me wanted to stretch so quickly it strained a tendon
and as for the other, with survival on her shoulder,
wanted to be more tender.
I would have known, if I had taken me on.
With the other half of me projected onto the empty seat
across from me,
I double dog dare her
to take us on.
We'll We'll
We'll.
We will till we're well.

Words I keep in my left boot
(on longs walks)
#8

The helicopter seeds fall on the sidewalk,
gathered in a zig-zag between the cracks.
Their small venue,
a concert.
There are no witnesses
but they keep on falling and playing and falling again
in private change.

Momma's Boy

Dissociation, you are my mother;
the breast I feed from,
the rest that I need from
these cubic grounds
and these atomic sounds.
I am anything but bound
by a roof or a cloud
or my two arched feet.
See, my feet, they arch to reach 10,000 ft.
They too would do anything to get off the ground.
You raised me like a momma's boy.

Dissociation, you are my mother.
And the real-world is my father.
And I spite him for his discomposure—
his fists, his hits, his post-work slaughter,
his beach babes that leech in his murky waters.
His lawyer shouldn't even bother
to make the custody joint.
But I must make the point
that he still holds custody around my joints—
my chronic pain, my muscle strain.
And for that I am a momma's boy.

Dissociation, you are my mother.

The overprotective kind, I'd say.

But you kept me alive, I'd say,

enough to wonder of the things I'll say

when I meet myself again someday.

Someday, will you let me move out of your basement?

and move into my body? It's for sale and it's vacant.

I promise, I'll make my payments.

I promise, I'll find my placement.

If not in the real-world, at least,

know that you raised me like a man of his word.

Dissociation, you are my mother.

So will you tuck me in at least once more, please,

and spook me with a scary story?

Of real-world men with gory glory.

Or persistent ones like Alcott's "Laurie".

Or distant ones that don't know to be sorry.

I've always been a homebody;

I rushed home when I crashed my car in one big spin.

I snuck home when my man, with a grin,

grabbed my neck and chin

with a little too much whim

like I was a dead duck to him.

And I knew home again at 8th grade's end,

when the world had its ends

as Revelation said.

And, mother, when there's another wildfire in my cells, yet again,

when I've used up my amens,

or love new men,

can I come home then?

You know you raised a prodigal son,

so let me be a momma's boy.

Sobao

The sobao bread is my same shade,
the same target.
Bread and wine,
body and the blood.
I'd tried to end my life
with a sandwich knife.
But a bee loses its sting
after the first strike.
So I butter sweet bread
and swallow the thought.

"I have had enough of burnt offerings of rams and the fat of well-fed beasts; I do not delight in the blood of bulls, or of lambs, or of goats"

Isaiah 1:11

Clements of Truth

This kitchen is full of citrus
and there's still some bitterness to me
but if someone's gonna have some
it's gotta be me.
My dog she lies with three good thighs
by the stove iron to make herself dry.
The rugs still soaked but I'll deal with it eventually,
right now, it's much too heavy.
On the stove there's a chicken thigh and it's been searing all
night.
I'll deal with it eventually
but right now, the scent burns too heavenly.
If these walls had better backbones, they'd say they were
ashamed of me.
If this plot of land could reach me, it'd say it couldn't blame
me
for the way that I've turned out to be.
I'm cuddled up in a straitjacket,
cause it's the closest thing I've got to having arms
wrapped tight around me
and I'll never let go of me. I'll never let go.

This might be erosion,
the way my weight has made the floors sink.
But the way I see it, this is how nature has meant it to be.

A house is nothing but a habitat,
and this wreckage brings me peace
because I can now respect its pieces
as pieces
to the way that I've turned out to be.
If there was someone to ask me, I'd say I'm proud of me.
I still don't say the Matador's name,
like a rejection of faith.
There is no quicker way to rattle the plates
or quiver the clock face
and I will bring no bad omens among this place.
But I always end up cursed, anyway.
Though, I swear I never swear.
But Jesus fucking Christ.
Some time I'll step outside
when I'm not so inward all the time
and guilt is not the cord that keeps me alive.
I'll deal with it eventually.
Right now, I look for irony.

The stove iron is burning
but I think I'll leave it be
because my dog, she's dry,
and the cold of night is returning
to this kitchen, full of citrus and bitterness.
The oranges burn to dust and powder up the kiwis.

Words I keep in my left boot
(on longs walks)
#9

The deer will see the roadway planted in his forest
and think that it's new soil
and that the vehicle is a wild boar.
The deer will greet it face to face
and meet its fate.

But the grass will overcome the sidewalk
as nature is ancient
and knows to come home.
The grass will swallow up the tiles of concrete
and they become its teeth.

Afterward

I was at a very angry stage in my life writing *The Matador's Wife*. This wasn't the violently autonomous, often misplaced teenage anger I was familiar with. This anger was steadfast. As I sat beside my youth from the sidelines, I watched every injustice and act of self-destruction unfold before me. I mourned for a version of myself that wasn't contrived of so many jagged edges. Like many budding adults, I felt a desperation to see myself as more than a history of my own making, as more than a past, as worthy of a future. But there is a terrifying kind of peace that comes with watching the foundations of all your belief systems crumble as you detach yourself from the disillusions of your youth. In a sense, *The Matador's Wife* is all about belief: belief in a person that believes far too much in themself, as well as the disbelief that comes with sitting beside yourself, absent of every role you know. It is also about the anger that can shift these beliefs. Because sometimes anger is the thing that kills. But sometimes it is the thing that saves.

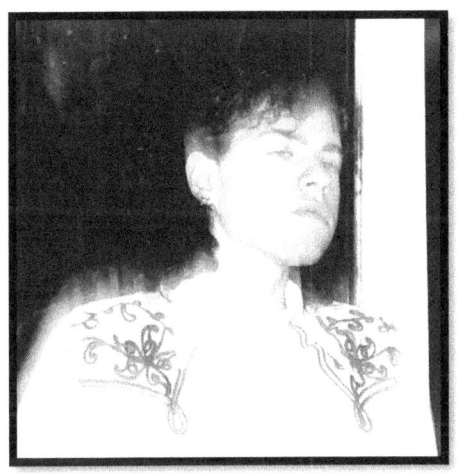

Andrés Colón is a young author, artist, writer, and graphic designer from Cincinnati, Ohio. Having self-published their first poetry book *Anatomy Of* at age 18, Andrés hopes to continue developing their craft to well represent their passionate generation. You can purchase *Anatomy Of* on Amazon in both eBook and paperback. Follow Andrés Colón throughout their creative journey on Instagram @a_ndres.c

Other Titles by Andrés Colón

Anatomy Of – A collection of art and poetry, available for purchase in eBook and paperback form on Amazon.

> "What are the stories that make up a person? And what faces does one wear when telling them? Sometimes these stories leave the teller with more questions than the listener, and the tellers of these tales would do anything for answers.

> *Anatomy Of* is a dissection of the self that starts with the brain, moves to the heart, and then into the lungs, utilizing the sharp tools of myth, fable, and folklore from around the world. Enhanced by vibrant photography and fantastical illustrations, *Anatomy Of* digs deep into themes of burnout, limerence, and self-sabotaging heroism."